W9-BJK-985

ONE

I watch movies on streaming services. There are so many interesting ones...

—ONE

Manga creator ONE began *One-Punch Man* as a webcomic, which quickly went viral, garnering over 10 million hits. In addition to *One-Punch Man*, ONE writes and draws the series *Mob Psycho 100* and *Makai no Ossan*.

YUSUKE MURATA

Never draw a line without purpose.

—Yusuke Murata

A highly decorated and skilled artist best known for his work on *Eyeshield 21*. Yusuke Murata won the 122nd Hop Step Award (1995) for *Partner* and placed second in the 51st Akatsuka Award (1998) for *Samui Hanashi*.

ONE-PUNCH MAN 23

ONE + YUSUKE MURATA

ONE-PUNCH MAN
23
STORY BY ONE
ART BY YUSUKE MURATA
AUTHENTICITY

CHARACTERS

STORY

A single man has arisen to face the evil threatening humankind! His name is Saitama, and he's become a hero for fun!

One day, a man named Garo shows up. He admires monsters, so he begins hero hunting. And around the same time, monsters calling themselves the Monster Association take a young boy named Waganma hostage and issue a challenge to the Hero Association, entering into a massive battle with them.

Even though he's still a child, Class-S hero Child Emperor is able to defeat the powerful monster known as Phoenix Man, and he and Waganma work to escape the underground base. Elsewhere, Bushi Drill and the other Class-A heroes on his team head for the surface with Narinki's private force, who've now been freed from Super S's control!

CONTENTS

23

[AUTHENTICITY]

PUNCH 107:
Back _____ 7

PUNCH 108:
Authenticity _____ 43

PUNCH 109:
A Dangerous Multiplying Monster _____ 73

PUNCH 110:
Love Evolution ____ 147

PUNCH 111:
Gluttony _____ 191

PUNCH 112:
Superalloy Blackluster _____ 203

BONUS MANGA:
Setting an Example _____ 219

PUNCH 107: BACK

HEH HEH HEH

HM ?
LOOK!

WHERE YOU CHUMPS GOIN'?
HEY!

ULLG... ORDERS FROM SUPER S...
MUST TAKE PRISONERS... TO GYORO-GYORO...
PLEASE! LET US GO!
MAMA!
OH, THE IGNO-MINY!
YOU HEROES ARE PITI-FUL!
HAW! GYORO-GYORO'S GONNA CUT YA, BURN YA AND TORTURE YA!
EEP!
BUT HE DON'T NEED ALL OF YA...
...SO I'LL JUST HAVE A LITTLE SNACK!
GWSH

SLASH
WHOK
SHING

!
THUD
THEY DIDN'T KNOW WE WERE FREE, AND THEY ATTACKED ANYWAY!
I THOUGHT IT WOULD WORK, BUT...
H
W
AM

KEH! YOU WUZ CRYIN', BUT NOW YOU WANNA FIGHT?!
AIN'T THEY BRAIN-WASHED ?!
KILL 'EM ALL AND RE-GROUP!
WE'LL HAVE TO FIGHT OUR WAY OUT!
HWUP
HWUP
URF!
WABAM

THIS TIME, VICTORY IS OURS!
WISH
?!
BLAM

SLAM
YOU GOT THAT RIGHT!
SPLAT
SPLAT
SPLAT

IF WE DON'T SAVE THE HOSTAGE, WE DON'T GET PAID.
OH.
UAAARGH!
SQUEEZ
GRAAH
THEY'RE GUTSY ...
AND WITH QUITE A GRUDGE.
WAP
WATCH OUT!
GUH!
KRCH
BAM

BLAM BLAM BLAM
CHAK
KTHUD
YOU SHOULD BE MORE CAREFUL.
IA!!
STANDING BEHIND ME IN BATTLE IS DANGEROUS.
WHAAAT?!
BUT WE'RE ON YOUR SIDE!!!
YOU'RE CAPTAIN, SO YOU BE CARE-FUL!

BAS
DID YOU THINK WE'D USE YOU AS A SHIELD?
THAT ISN'T OUR STYLE.
DON'T DIS-RESPECT US.
BLAM
BLA-BLAM
...BUT IT'S INGRAINED IN ME.
SORRY ...
...

REGULAR TROOPS USE MERCENARIES AS SHIELDS...
...AND SOMETIMES THE PEOPLE WE TRY TO SAVE TURN OUT TO BE THE ENEMY IN DISGUISE.
YOU HEROES HAVE NO IDEA OF THE HORROR...
TWCH TWCH
YOU STILL SHOULDN'T HAVE HIT HIM.
I'LL BE MORE CARE-FUL.
MY APOLO-GIES.
Um, okay...
...
MERCE-NARIES WILL DO ANYTHING FOR MONEY.
...

IT'S POSSIBLE HE'S USED HIS OWN COMRADES AS SHIELDS.
BEST NOT TO PUT TOO MUCH TRUST IN HIM...
YOU! WITH THE BEARD!
ME?
I NOTICED ...
...YOU WOULDN'T EVEN FAKE CRY.
WE JUST GOTTA GET BACK ALIVE ...
...SO SWALLOW YOUR PRIDE.
WE SAVED HIS BACON AND HE'S ACTING SUPERIOR ?!

SHK
SOME-THING'S BENEATH US!
GAGH!

KA SHASH
ON IT!
KEEP FIGHTING UP THERE!

STAGGER
KRUMBL
KRUMBL

!

YOU COME LIKE MOTHS TO A FLAME...

KI-OO
M

...FOR MY HAIR TO ENSNARE YOU!
Threat Level: Demon
MALONG HAIR

A HOT DUDE!
GULP
...
THAT HAIR IS A WEAPON ...

IT IS FORBIDDEN LOVE!!!
BUT HE'S A MONSTER, AND I'M A HERO!
HE'S FLIRTING WITH ME!
BA BUMP

GET A GRIP, YOU FOOL!
HE FELL FOR A MONSTER AGAIN.

UM, KAMA ?
BABUMP

...SO TEST HIM WITH YOUR FLYING SWORD.
KAMA, WE DON'T KNOW THAT HAIR'S RANGE OR POWERS...

CALM DOWN AND STOP MESSING AROUND!
...
MAY I STRIKE HIM DOWN?
HUH?
ARE YOU JEALOUS?
HEY ...
WHO'RE YOU CALLING A FOOL ?!
WE NEED TO COMPLETE THE RESCUE AND GET BACK...
OUR JOB AS BACKUP IS TO LIGHTEN THE BURDEN ON MASTER AND THE OTHERS!
...OR WE CAN NEVER FACE MASTER AGAIN! WHILE WE'RE WASTING TIME, THE BATTLE RAGES ON FOR THE OTHERS!
GURK!
SLASH

ドゴゴゴ

UNDER-STOOD.
HE'S A HOTTIE, BUT THERE'S NO CHOICE.
I'M SORRY ...
...BUT I CANNOT RETURN YOUR FEELINGS !!!
REJEC-TION STRIKES ...
... LIKE A BOLT FROM THE BLUE.
SHWOOO
FLYING SWORD!

FWIP
WOOSH
SLICING THROUGH THE AIR CREATES A GIANT WHIRLWIND.
I HATE TO ADMIT IT, BUT IT IS BEYOND MY ABILITIES!
LIKE FROGS IN A WELL, YOU ARE IGNORANT ...

...FOR MY MANE IS STRON-GER THAN YOU THINK!
SKIP
BUT WHAT'S WITH THE DUMB SIMILES?
IMPOSSIBLE! HE BLOCKED IT WITH HIS LONG HAIR!

KAMA!
BEHIND YOU! UNDER-GROUND!
!
WHSH
SLASH
FLUSH

BWS!
WHAT A PAIN.
HWIP
TCH!
TOMP
TH-THANKS ...
PFOO
THAT HAIR...
IT'S THIN, SO IT PENETRATES WHERE BLADES CAN'T!

DON'T LOSE SIGHT OF A SINGLE STRAND!
WE MUST PREVENT AN ATTACK FROM ABOVE.
... THIS MONSTER GET PAST US!
WE CAN'T LET...

BWSH

DON'T TRY FOL-LOWING THEM WITH YOUR EYES!
FOOF

...WITH PURE REFLEXES!
COUNTER THE HAIR'S MURDEROUS INTENT...
LIKE SALT IN YOUR WOUNDS...
...SUFFER MY LONG HAIR!

THE HUMAN HEAD HAS OVER 100,000 HAIRS!
BUT WE ONLY HAVE THREE SWORDS!
MISSING ONE STRAND MEANS DEATH! SO BLOCK THEM ALL!
IF YOU FALTER, THEY'LL SPEAR YOUR INTERNAL ORGANS!
THIS IS GONNA WEAR ON OUR NERVES ...
FWIFF
URGH!
GRIK
SWING
SLASH

SHUNK
IT JUST KEEPS COMING!

BUMP

BESIDES ...

WE CAN SENSE MALICE, SO WE CAN DODGE ATTACKS FROM ALL SIDES.
YES, BUT WE'RE WELL SUITED FOR THIS FIGHT.

WE HAVE EACH OTHER TO LEAN ON!

...
THAT'S RIGHT.
WHAT THE?
WHAT'S GOTTEN INTO YOU?
HAVE YOU FALLEN FOR ME AGAIN?
I NEVER DID!

HMPH!
YOU HAVE THE WORST LINES...
LIKE CANDLES IN THE WIND...
...SO ARE YOUR LIVES.
SHOOSH

WE NEED TO CUT THROUGH IT ALL TO GET CLOSE!
IT'S TIME FOR A HAIR-CUT!
LOP OFF ALL 100,000 STRANDS!
GRAH!

STOP, YOU!
DMP
DMP
DMP
DMP
ARGH! THOSE PESTS!

...

?!
CHOMP
MNCH
MNCH

SWIP

MUNCH
MUNCH

SNEAK
IS SOME-THING THERE?

CHOMP
W-WHAT WAS THAT SOUND?
MUNCH
CHOMP
CHOMP

DON'T GO THAT WAY!
CARE-FUL!
SHHH!
THERE'S A SCARY MONSTER!
CHOMP
CHOMP
BU
SLURP
CRUNCH

26 yrs.
37 yrs.
23 yrs.

PUNCH 108: AUTHENTICITY

HUFF
HUFF
HUFF

MY ACHILLES' HEEL IS...
...MY HAIR.

THUD

YOU STILL BREATHIN'?!
WE'RE DONE UP HERE!

HUFF
HUFF
THAT'S RIGHT ...
WITH GREATER NUMBERS AND REACH, HE TRULY WAS A MENACING AND HORRIFYING OPPONENT.

DID WE WIN?
HUFF
BUT ALL WE DID WAS CUT HIS AT-TACKING HAIR!
HUFF

WELL, I'M SURE MASTER WILL BE FINE.
THE THREE OF US BARELY SUR-VIVED.
ONE BLADE WOULD NOT HAVE BEEN ENOUGH.
ARE THERE MORE LIKE HIM? THIS COULD GET ROUGH!

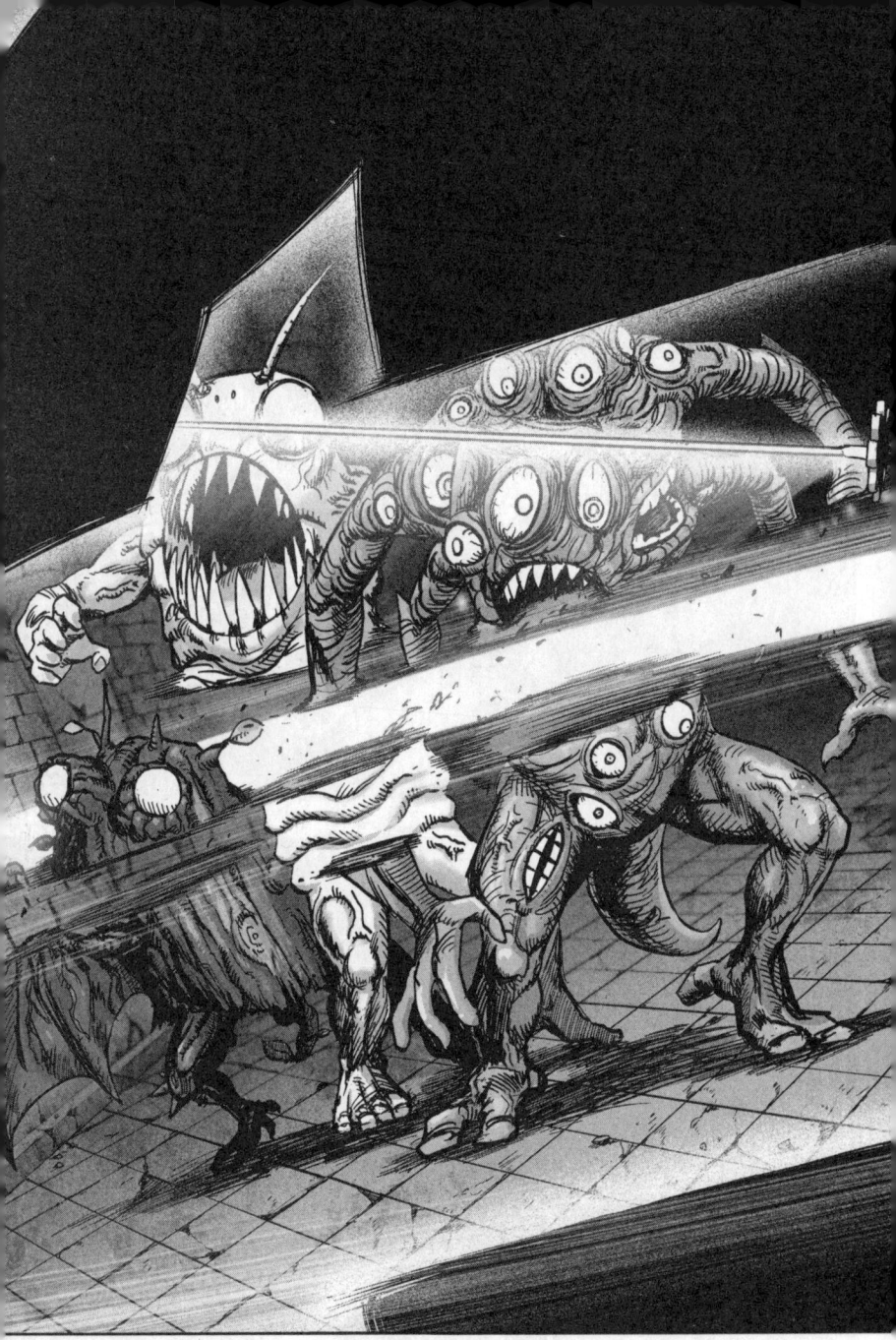

KA
SPLAT
DID SOME-ONE ESCAPE MY BLADE?
YOU ARE INDEED A MASTER, ATOMIC SAMURAI!
TSHHH
!
YOU LURE THEM IN AND SLASH THEM ALL IN ONE STRIKE!

KLOMP
I WILL FEAST ON YOUR BLOOD AND REIGN UN-MATCHED!
I OFFERED MY SOUL TO MY BLADE AND BECAME THE SWORD DEMON KNOWN AS THE CHOPPER-UPPER!
GWAAAAAR!
BAM BAM
BAM BAM

SPLAT
IS ANY-ONE LEFT? RAISE YOUR HAND.
ALL RIGHT, IS THAT ALL?
URGH ...
WE'RE EVEN!
!!!
KLINK

KAA
SHANK
I AM MACHINE GOD GS...
...AND I HAVE COLLECTED BATTLE DATA ON ATOMIC SAMURAI.
NOW I CAN COPY YOUR EVERY SWORD STROKE.
RESISTANCE IS FUTILE, SO OFFER ME YOUR NECK!

ARE YOU COPYING MY MOVES?
IM-PRESSIVE. TOYS THESE DAYS ARE SO WELL-MADE.

I GOTTA ORDER ONE OFF THE INTERNET TO HELP MY PUPILS TRAIN.

BRING IT ON.

WHG
ATOMIC
SLASH!
SLAH

TWO-
BLADE
STYLE!
ASH

JUST A CHEAP IMITATION, HUH?
KABOOM

BOOM
BUT HIS CORE WAS SO HARD I COULDN'T CUT IT...
A LAST-DITCH ATTACK, HUH?!
YOU ARE SUCH A SORE LOSER!
FLYING SWORD!

SLICE
KCHINK
THEY'VE GOT SKILLS TOO.
WELL, THE SURFACE TEAM CAN HANDLE HIM.
TCH... HE GOT AWAY.

AND THEY'RE BETTER AT TEAMWORK.
SWIP SWIP
HM ...
SLASH
YOU REALLY ARE CLASS A!
I LIKE YOUR SKILLS!
FWUD
I OWE IT TO MASTER'S TEACHING.
SHNK

WANNA WORK FOR OUR PMC?
I CAN GET YOU GOOD JOBS WITH BETTER PAY.
PMC: PRIVATE MILITARY COMPANY

AND I CAN RECOM-MEND A PROS-THETICS MAKER WE FUND.
Business Card

OH...

TRANS-FERRING ISN'T AN OPTION.
THANKS, BUT BEING HEROES IS PART OF HOW WE TRAIN.

ACTUALLY, THEY'RE A FORM OF SELF-DISCIPLINE.
YOU REALLY TOOK THE FIGHT OUT OF THOSE MONSTERS.
FOR SURPRISE ATTACKS.
WE COULD USE SKILLS LIKE THAT.
...
HOW ABOUT YOU BECOME SWORDSMEN OR HEROES?
HMM...
BUSHIDO AND FIGHTING FOR JUSTICE ARE TOO MUCH TROUBLE.
NO CAN DO.

BUT I COULD TEACH YOU A THING OR TWO...
...ABOUT THE DARKEST ASPECTS OF HUMAN NATURE.
...
I'LL KEEP THAT IN MIND.
YOU KNOW, IF YOU JOINED US, I COULD TEACH YOU HOW TO FAKE CRY.
NEVER!
MY CREW WEEPS LIKE REAL THESPIANS!
Hmm...
HM?

I EVEN PEED A LITTLE!
IT WAS NECESSARY IN ORDER TO FIND AN OPENING.
SERIOUSLY? I WAS BAWLING MY HEAD OFF!
THANKS TO YOU, WE SURVIVED.
NO WAY! EVERYONE WAS FAKING?!
BUT CAPTAIN, YOU'RE BEST AT IT.
WE HEROES COULD LEARN FROM THEM.
THEY EXCEL AT TEAMWORK.
THEN I'LL PRETEND I WAS ALSO FAKING.
ANYWAY, CLEVER RUSE!
NO ONE WAS CRYING FOR REAL?

TIP TIP TIP TIP
TROMP
TROMP
WAIT!
HELP, HELP, HELP, HELP! GYAiEEE!

TROMP
I'LL JUST KILL YOU! REAL FAST! THEN IT'LL BE OVER!
I WON'T HURT YOU!
TROMP
HEY, BOY!
STOP RIGHT THERE!
TROMP
TROMP
Threat Level: Dragon
BLACK SPERMATOZOON

PSHO
UM

HWUP

HEY...
...YOU'VE GOT MOVES.

PUNCH 109:
A DANGEROUS MULTIPLYING MONSTER

Five minutes earlier...
DON'T LET EVEN ONE ESCAPE!
WAA
怪人出没注意

GRAAAW!
AMBUSHIN' US OUTSIDE WAS COWARDLY!
SLASH
BUT SINCE YOU'RE JUST THE B-TEAM–
LIKE YOU CAN TALK!
UMF!
KRAK
GYA!!

OH, HEY!
!
WHOMP
WHAM
WHOK WHOK WHOK
FWIP
RUSTL RUSTL
YOU GOT IT!
I FOUND AN EXIT!
PLUG IT, GREEN!
...WILL COME UP THROUGH THAT MANHOLE SOON.
AND THE ATTACK TEAM...
RUSTL RUSTL
SLUP
NOW WE'VE CLOSED MOST OF THEIR EXITS.

I SURE HOPE CHILD EMPEROR HAS WAGANMA!
WHOA!
WHAT JUST HAP-PENED ?!
RMBL RMBL RMBL
BOOM
THOOM

KA-SLAM
EVERY HERO DOWN THERE WILL DIE!
FOOLS!
NO ONE CAN ESCAPE OROCHI'S TENTA-CLES!
Threat Level: Demon
BUILDING BLASTER
PWA HA HA!
HE BLOCKED THE MAN-HOLE!

ARF! ARF!
UP THERE!
IT'S OUR WAY OUT!
YAHOO!
BUT IS IT SAFE? I HEARD A LOUD NOISE.
THE SURFACE TEAM MAY BE ENGAGING FLEEING MONSTERS.
HM ?
WHAT ?!
PUSH
PUSH
HNNNGH!
PUSH
IT WON'T OPEN!
IS IT RUSTED SHUT?!
HUUUH?!
LET'S ALL PUSH TOGETHER!

KA BOOM
BA BOOM
IDJITS! YOU THOUGHT YOU'D TRAPPED US, BUT NOW YOUR COMRADES ARE DOOMED!
PWA HA HA!
KSHUNK
KSHUNK
ONE, TWO ...
I'LL INFORM CHILD EMPEROR!
THEN GET TO IT!
YES, BUT IT'LL TAKE TIME! LIKE 30 MINUTES?
PATTA PATTA
GREEN! CAN YOU MAKE ANOTHER WAY OUT?!

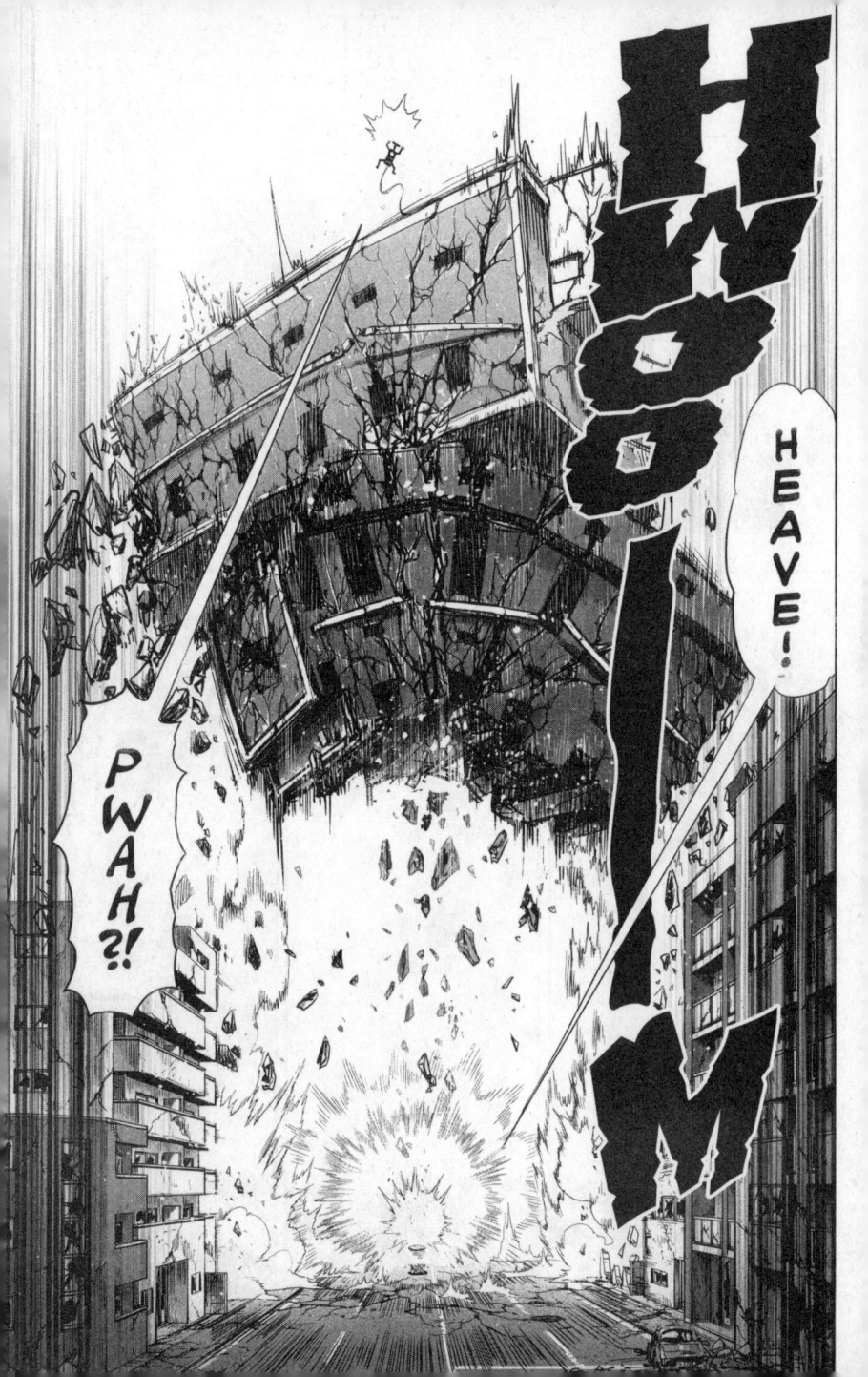
HWOOOIN
HEAVE!
PWAH?!

YAIIII...
...
KATHOO—M

IT OPENED!
PEEK
KLUNK
CHILD EMPER-OR!

GASP
W-WE GOT OUT!
YOU RES-CUED WAGAN-MA!

H-HOW DID YOU DO THAT?
WHAT?
THE MAN-HOLE?

WELL, IT WAS A BIT RUSTY...
...SO IT NEEDED A LITTLE OOMPH.

THAT WAS A LITTLE OOMPH?!
DID HE USE SOME KIND OF INVEN-TION?
WHAT A KID!

CLASS S ALWAYS IMPRESS-ES!
?

PLONK

KTINK

GOOD BOY! I'LL GIVE YOU A BONE-SHAPED BATTERY LATER.
ARF!
YAY
ANYWAY, THE MISSION IS A SUC-CESS!

DID THE MON-STERS TAKE YOU HOSTAGE ?!

I RESCUED HIM DOWN BELOW.
HE'S A HERO TOO.

Huh? Bounty hunters?!
WHO'S THAT?

NAH. IT WAS NOISY, SO I WENT DOWN THERE TO COMPLAIN.
YOU'RE SUP-POSED TO BE A HERO. GET OUT OF MY SIGHT!
Take it easy...
WHAT IF I HAD TO SEND A RESCUE TEAM?!
!!!

I BLOCKED THE MONSTER TUNNELS THAT WAY, SO IT'S SAFE. JUST TURN LEFT AND FOLLOW THE HIGHWAY.
SEE YA!
TCH... OKAY, OKAY!

I JUST WANNA GET THIS OVER WITH!
WHAT A PAIN!
UNK
GR

KTO
OOM

THE RESCUE WAS A SUCCESS!
I REPEAT! THE RESCUE WAS A SUCCESS!
THIS IS CHILD EMPEROR! I'VE RE-JOINED THE SURFACE TEAM!
!
THIS IS ZOMBIE-MAN!
GOOD WORK...
...CHILD EMPEROR!

ZOMBIEMAN...

CHOMP CHOMP
ALL'S WELL HERE!
WHAT?
MUNCH MUNCH
THIS IS....
CHOMP CHOMP
CHILD...
WHO IS THAT? IT'S TOO NOISY!

THIS IS AMAI MASK! COPY ON THE HOSTAGE!
THESE MONSTERS ARE A CINCH!
I WILL CONTINUE TO ADMINISTER JUSTICE!

A CHILD?
I'M BUSY ON A LOWER FLOOR, BUT I FOUND A CHILD DOWN HERE!
UM... THIS IS ATOMIC SAMURAI!

GULP
I'M DIGESTING LIKE CRAZY!
OH... IT'S PIG GOD.

HE'S STILL ALIVE?
BA BMP
BA BMP
IT MUST BE TAREO.
GACK

AGH!
HELLO ?!
MY LOCATION IS... WHERE AM I AGAIN? ANYWAY, I'LL GO IN PURSUIT!
I THOUGHT IT MIGHT BE A CHILD MONSTER, BUT A SMALL BLACK MONSTER WAS CHASING HIM AROUND, SO HE'S PROBABLY HUMAN.

WE GOT CUT OFF ...
WHAT CHILD ?!
THIS IS CHILD EMPEROR!

IT'S VAST DOWN THERE, SO THERE MUST BE MANY CELLS...
...
BA BMP
BA BMP
H- HEY, GO RESCUE HIM!
HUH ?!
N- NO... WE, UH...
POISON
TUMP
I HAVE TO GO BACK IN.
WHAT ?!
NO, DON'T! YOU USED YOUR ULTIMATE WEAPON FOR ME!
LEAVE IT TO THE ADULTS ALREADY DOWN THERE!
I CAN'T DO THAT.

I'M THE ONLY ONE WHO CAN ANALYZE THE ENEMY TECH AND SHARE HOW TO BEAT IT.
BESIDES, I STILL HAVE SOME SECRET WEAPONS.
WELL, WE CAN'T LET THE TYKE GO ALONE!
YEAH, WE'LL JOIN YOU!
NO, THAT ISN'T NECES-SARY.
BESIDES, SOMEONE HAS TO GUARD THE SURFACE.
WE EACH HAVE A ROLE TO PLAY.
SO...

HE'S TUBBY WITH THICK LIPS AND A UNIBROW, AND HE HAS A BOWL CUT WITH A LITTLE BALD SPOT, AND HE'S WEARING A SHIRT THAT SAYS "BG" ON IT.
UM... HIS NAME IS TAREO.

HE WAS IN MY CELL...
...BUT A MONSTER TOOK HIM AWAY.
I DIDN'T SAY ANYTHING BECAUSE I DIDN'T WANT YOU TO GO BACK FOR HIM.
I WAS TOO SCARED.

SORRY...
JOLT
PAT
HUH?
THANKS FOR TELLING ME.
NOW GOOD LUCK!

GAKLUNK
...I WANT TO MAKE CLASS S, BUT IT'S A HIGH HURDLE TO JUMP!
SOME-DAY...

GLW
ATOMIC SAMURAI COMETH! THE HARD-BOILED HERO WITH A WARM HEART!
YOU TRIED TO CUT ME. ARE YOU PICKING A FIGHT?
"COMETH"? GIVE ME A BREAK.
ATOMIC SAMURAI, HUH? GYORO-GYORO MEN-TIONED YOU.
YOU DON'T LOOK LIKE MUCH, BUT OH WELL.
I GOT BORED WAITING FOR YOU, SO MAKE THIS FUN.
WHAT-EVER ...
BUT WHAT'S IN IT FOR ME?

YOU ARE ...
... LOOK-ING DOWN ON ME.
WUP

BULLGE
SNAP
POP

NAH!
THIS'LL BE AN EASY VIC-TORY.
YOU SHOULD TAKE ME...
... MORE SERI-OUSLY.
SWISH

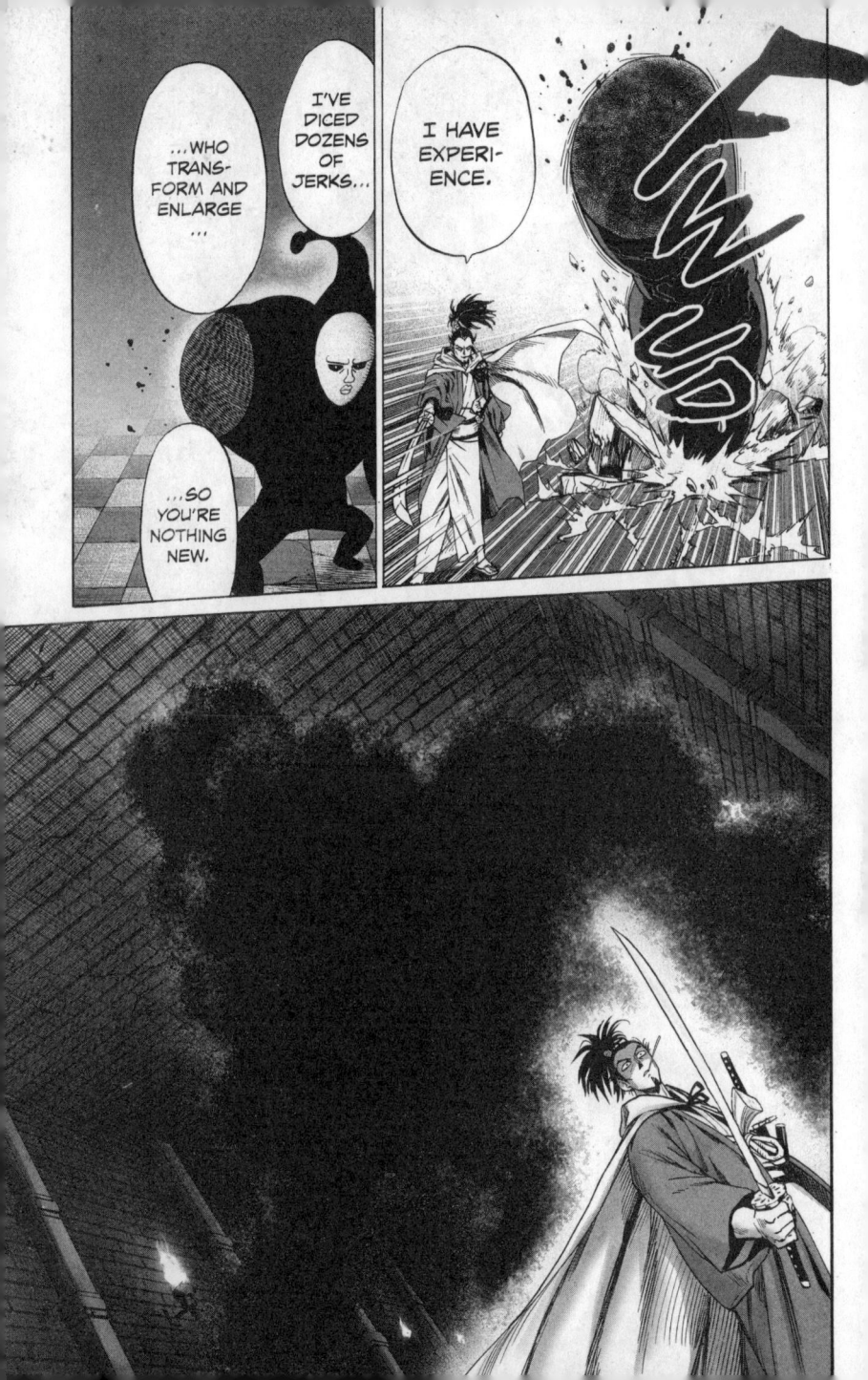
I'VE DICED DOZENS OF JERKS...
...WHO TRANS-FORM AND ENLARGE ...
...SO YOU'RE NOTHING NEW.
I HAVE EXPERI-ENCE.
FWUD

CRIK
SNAP
CRAK

YOU CAN DIVIDE, HUH?
TCH...
HOW PESKY.

PESKY?
ARE YOU STUPID?

YOU STILL THINK YOU CAN WIN?
I'M A MASS OF COUNT-LESS SELVES.

PLOOP LOOP LOOP LOOP LOOP
...AND I WILL ONLY MULTI-PLY!
CUT, REND, HIT, CRUSH AND BREAK ME...

YOU'RE THE DUMB ONE!
I'LL MERELY CUT YOU COUNT-LESS TIMES!
GO ON, DO IT!
I'LL MAKE YOU WEEP!
C'MON, BRING IT.
LET'S DO THIS.
SLASH!

ドガッ

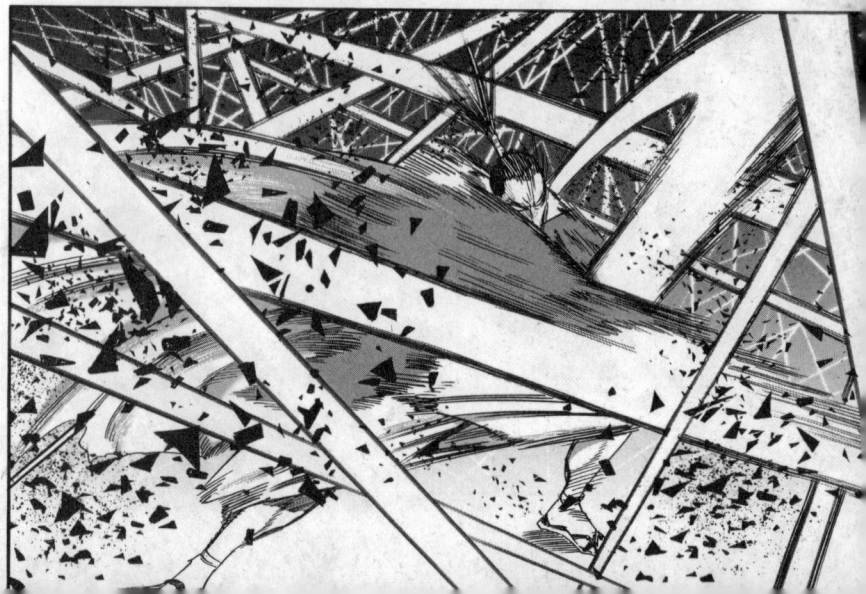

FLIP
FLIP
FLIP
FLIP

ATOMIC
...

SLASH!

WELCOME ...
...TO YOUR DOOM!

KA
BIM
KOFF!
WHAT THE?!
THIS MONSTER DIVIDED ...
...BUT HE'S STILL INCREDIBLY POWERFUL!
I UNDERESTIMATED HIS STRENGTH!
THIS IS BAD!
THERE'S TOO MANY OF HIM !!!

BA BAM BAM
I CAN'T-
BAM BAM
KASLAN
KA BAM-
BAM
BAM BAM BAM

SETHE
SETHE
SETHE
SETHE
SO WISE UP!
SERI-OUSLY, IT'S NO USE.

WE'RE THE WORST TYPE OF OPPONENT FOR YOU!
GYORO-GYORO FIGURED THAT OUT ALREADY!

KRAKK
KEH!
I'LL BURY YOU!
BAM
THE CEIL-ING ?!

KATHOOM
DADOOM
WHAT'S ALL THIS SHAKING?
KRUMBL KRUMBL
I WONDER HOW THE BATTLE IS GOING ...

OH, ARE YOU WORRIED ...
...ABOUT HOW YOUR PEERS ARE DYING?

!
BWAH
WHERE DID HE COME FROM?!
MAYBE THEY DIED LIKE THIS!

DIE BEFORE YOU CAN EVEN RESIST!
DA SHOOM
RMM
FNAP
FNAP

Threat Level: Dragon

THE HOMELESS EMPEROR

WOOOO
I SAW THE HERO ASSOCIATION WEBSITE. THE NUMBER OF CLASS-S HEROES...
TUMP
IS THAT HOW A HERO DIES? WHAT A LETDOWN.
WAIT ...
...IS ONE I CAN ELIMINATE ALL ON MY OWN!

WHSH
THOK
BOOM

FUMP
!
KLCK

BZZA
KKKK
SPLAT

SSSLUMP
THAT LOOKS PAINFUL.
GLORP
HE BLOCKED AT THAT RANGE?!

GWUMP
TCH... I WAS SAVING THIS, BUT...
SCHWUP
SPINNN
DRRIP
SCHNAP
KA
KCH

KEBOM

FSH
OOO
M

INDEED, YOU WERE A TOP HERO.
RMM

EVEN DEATH DIDN'T STOP YOU...
...SO YOU MUST HAVE BEEN STRONG.
RMM

HEY.
YOUR ATTACKS ARE LIKE MAGIC, AND THAT'S NOT FAIR.
THAT MONSTER IS SERIOUSLY POWERFUL.
WHAT'S YOUR DEAL?
PWAH
...THE SECRET OF THIS LIGHT'S POWER?
YOU WANT TO KNOW ...
THEY SAID YOU COULDN'T DIE, BUT I THOUGHT THEY MEANT FIGURATIVELY.
I'M SURPRISED. THE NAME ZOMBIEMAN ACTUALLY SUITS YOU.

VERY WELL. I WILL RELATE HOW I ACQUIRED MY POWERS.
UNTIL A MONTH AGO, I LIVED IN THE PARK.
I LOST MY JOB AND MY HOUSE...
...AND WITH-DREW FROM SOCIETY FOR A LIFE OF SECLUSION.
AT A WELCOME PARTY FOR NEW EMPLOYEES, MY BOSS ORDERED ME TO DANCE NAKED..
...AND THE NEXT DAY I GOT FIRED FOR SEXUAL HARASSMENT.

HUMAN BEINGS ARE INSIGNIFICANT COMPARED TO THE PLANET SURROUNDING THEM.
THE LAND IS BIGGER THAN ANY BUILDING AND THE SKY BRIGHTER THAN ANY ARTIFICIAL LIGHT.
MY HOME WAS THE EARTH, MORE SPACIOUS THAN ANY MANSION.
AND THEN I REALIZED SOMETHING...
BUT WHEN I LOOKED UP AT THE SKY, MY HATRED FOR MY BOSS DIDN'T MATTER.
KEEP OFF

HUMANS ARE FOOLISH TO REMOVE THEMSELVES FROM THE GREAT WEB OF LIFE...
...IN ORDER TO SELFISHLY FLOURISH ACCORDING TO THEIR OWN DESIGNS.
THE WORLD IS AWFUL!
THOSE FOOLS TREATED ME LIKE SCUM!
IT'S UNBEAR-ABLE!

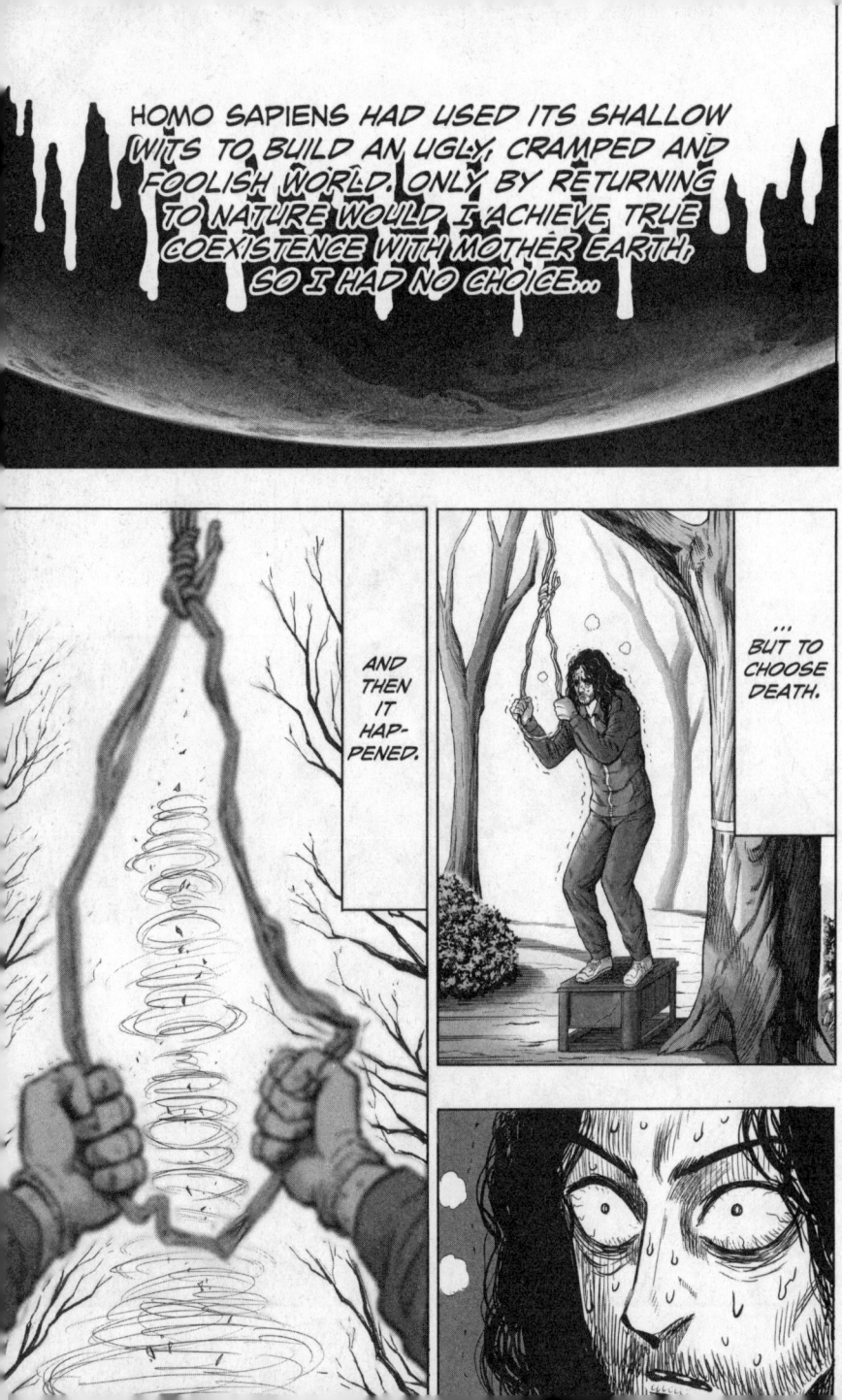
HOMO SAPIENS HAD USED ITS SHALLOW WITS TO BUILD AN UGLY, CRAMPED AND FOOLISH WORLD. ONLY BY RETURNING TO NATURE WOULD I ACHIEVE TRUE COEXISTENCE WITH MOTHER EARTH, SO I HAD NO CHOICE...
AND THEN IT HAP-PENED.
...BUT TO CHOOSE DEATH.

GOD APPEARED BEFORE MY EYES.

I WILL GRANT YOU POWER!
HUMAN BEINGS ARE FOOLS.
BUT YOU DO NOT NEED TO DIE.
YOU ARE CORRECT.
...WITH THAT POWER.
AND YOU KNOW WHAT YOU SHOULD DO...

THUS, I WIELD DIVINE POWER FROM GOD!
GOD CHOSE ME BECAUSE I KNOW THE SOLUTION.
FOOLISH HUMANS ARE A PLAGUE UPON THE EARTH...
...SO I WILL DESTROY THEIR CIVILIZATION AND THEIR VERY EXISTENCE!
UH-OH ...
WHY DO YOU BELIEVE THAT THING WAS GOD?
DID IT HAVE SOME KIND OF I.D.?
HIS STORY ENDED BEFORE I COULD FULLY REGEN-ERATE.

YOU DO NOT NEED TO BELIEVE IN GOD, SO ENOUGH WITH THE BANTER!

WAH
ATONE FOR YOUR ARROGANCE BY DYING AND RETURNING TO DUST!
RUMBLE
IS THE GROUND ALL RIGHT HERE?
RUMBLE
I HOPE MY PLACE IS OKAY!
TUMP
TUMP

PUNCH 110:
LOVE EVOLUTION
ANCHOR BATO

FZAM
TAIONKTONK
LOVE LIGHTNING SESSION!
CRAKL CRAKL
AWESOME!
MAIKO-PLASMA!
HIGH VOLTAGE MODE!

ZA
TAKE THAT!
Ko
oo
m

FWOOO

DID WE BEAT HIM?

FSHHHH
WHAT'S WITH THAT POSE?!
...?!
MAYBE HE ISN'T HUMAN!
BUT GYORO-GYORO SAID WE COULD WIN THIS!
CLASS S AND CLASS A ARE TOTALLY DIFFERENT!
CLASS S/A
WHOA... EVEN THIS MODE DIDN'T WORK!
Electric Catfish Man Plate Tectonics Mode

WE'VE USED ELECTRICITY ...
... PARASITIC EGGS...
... FREEZING ...

...ANES-THETIC GAS...
...HEAT...
...AND VENOM.
...ULTRA-SONIC SOUND...

WHY SO SUR-PRISED ?
WHAT MAKES HIM SO STRONG ?!
BUT NOTHING HAS WORKED!
IT'S BE-CAUSE I HAVE LOVE AS DEEP AS THE SEA WITH WHICH TO EMBRACE THE PAIN.
I CALL IT THE ANGEL ☆ HUG!
....!
PWING
WHAT THE?! WE'LL NEVER BEAT HIM!
I DON'T GET IT.

TEM-
PORARY
RETREAT!
!
DMP
DMP
DMP
DMP
WHERE
ARE YOU
GOING?
DMP
DMP
DMP
DMP
!!!

OROCHI AND GYORO-GYORO WOULD NEVER APPROVE OF RUNNING AWAY.
Threat Level: Demon
VACUUMER
YEAH! GO RIGHT AHEAD!
AW, SHUD-DUP! FIGHT 'IM ALONE IF YOU WANT, VACUUMER!
BUT FIRST, I WANT YOUR POWERS!
I THINK I WILL.
SNP

SKID
RMBL
RMBL
RMBL
RMBL
HM ?!
SHLORMP
YIKES!
GYAAH!
WHOA!
GWOOSH

AGH!
GWOC
HONEY!
DON'T LET GO!
A MONSTER KILLING MONSTERS?!
SLORMP
MAI-KO!
KYAAAH!
YOU HAVE NO LOVE ...
...FOR YOUR MATES.
BAM
NOOO!

HOO HOO HOO!
I'VE FINISHED MY APPETIZERS ...
NOW FOR THE MAIN COURSE!
BANG

BWOOM
I HAVE THE ABILITY TO DIGEST AND USE SUPERPOWERS UNTIL I EXCRETE THEM!
THAT'S ALL I NEED TO DESTROY YOU HEROES ...
...AND STEAL YOUR POWERS TOO!

DESTROY THE HEROES? YOU COULD *NEVER* BEAT THEM.

KR-KK

EVEN A CLASS-S HERO LIKE ME BARELY COMPARES!

SZZZZZ

I'M JUST A NORMAL DUDE!

UAGH!
BWOOF
THOUM
YOU AREN'T AVERAGE. YOU'RE MONSTROUS!

YOU BELIEVED YOU HAD EMBRACED THE ELECTRICITY AND POISON...
...BUT THOSE ATTACKS HAVE TAKEN THEIR TOLL!
TRMBL
TRMBL
TRMBL
TRMBL
TRMBL
TRMBL
TRMBL
TRMBL

HMPH!
YOUR BODY CRIES OUT IN PAIN.

HM?
I CAN SEE YOU TREMBLING.

...
YOUR SPIRIT MAY BE STRONG, BUT YOUR BODY CAN'T KEEP UP!
HOO HOO HOO HOO !!!
TCH
HOO HOO HOO HOO!

KRA
KK
KTHOOM

BVVVV
MY LOVE HAS GIVEN BIRTH TO A NEW STYLE!
WHAT IS THAT?!
W-WHAT DID YOU JUST DO?
...?!
?!
BVV...
DESCENDED!!!
VIBRATION ☆ ANGEL...
VVV
HUH???

BVOOSH
VIBRA-TION ☆ DARK ☆ ANGEL ☆ RUSH !!!

YOU TRULY *ARE* A MONSTER!
YOU ...

GUH!
THUD
OOF!
FWUD

BUT WON'T WE BE PUNISHED FOR FLEEING ?!

WE'RE GETTING OUTTA HERE!
HUH ?!

HONEY!
WHSH

EVEN MONSTERS TREAT HIM LIKE A MONSTER.
KLOMP
WHOA ...

LIKE AN EARTHQUAKE!
WHO CARES?! MY WHISKERS SENSE SOMETHING BIG COMING!

BUT TODAY HE DIES.
THE RAZOR BROKE AGAINST HIS THROAT!
WE TRIED OFFIN' HIM IN HIS BUNK, BUT IT DIDN'T WORK!
THAT VOICE ...
PREPARE YOURSELF, BOSS O' DA STINK SLAMMER!
I MEAN, PURI-PURI PRISONER! CUZ WE'RE YER ENEMIES !!!
AND IT'S REVENGE TIME!!!
RMBL RMBL RMBL RMB

LIKE YOU CAN TALK!
YOU LOOK LIKE MONSTERS!
HRAH
WAIT FOR ME! I WILL SAVE YOU!
DARN THAT MONSTER ASSOCIATION! IT SHOULDN'T PICK ON WEAK BOYS!
OH, MY HONEYS!
THE ONES A MONSTER TOOK AWAY!
WHY DO YOU LOOK LIKE THAT?!
FWAM
BAM
EVERY WORD YOU SAY IS INFURIATING!
WHAM WHOK
WHO YOU CALLIN' WEAK?!
WHAM
KRAK
WEEP AND SCREAM!
GET 'IM, GUYS!

WE'RE ALSO GONNA MURDER ALL YER BUDDIES AND THE GUARDS BACK IN THE JOINT!
DON'T THINK THIS IS ENOUGH TO SATIFY US!
WHAM
THOK
RIP OUT HIS HEART !!!
FLAY 'IM!
MONSTER-IZATION HAS JADED YOUR HEARTS!
THIS IS AWFUL!
THAT CAN'T BE! WE ATE TOGETHER! SLEPT TOGETHER! LABORED TOGETHER!
OUR HEARTS COMMUNED IN LOVE! REMEMBER THOSE DAYS OF SPLENDOR!
GWAH
OPEN YOUR EYES!
UWAH!

GET IT THROUGH YER THICK SKULL!!!
YOU ALWAYS SKIPPED PENAL LABOR ANYWAY!
WE DO! AND IT MAKES OUR BLOOD BOIL!!!
LET ME TEACH YOU SOME-THING.
NO, UM...
GWAH
JUST TRUST IN ME, AND I WILL SAVE YOU!
THE MON-STERIZED WILL NEVER AGAIN BE HUMAN.

TOO BAD, HUH?
GWAH!

CAT-
STIGA-
TION!
ガリガリ

Threat Level: Dragon

NYAAN

SO
RRT

THE REST IS ON YOU GUYS.
STAGGER
MY SWEATER! THE ONE MY BOY-FRIEND KNITTED!
TMP TMP

THE BIG SHOT'S SUPER TOUGH...
WOW...

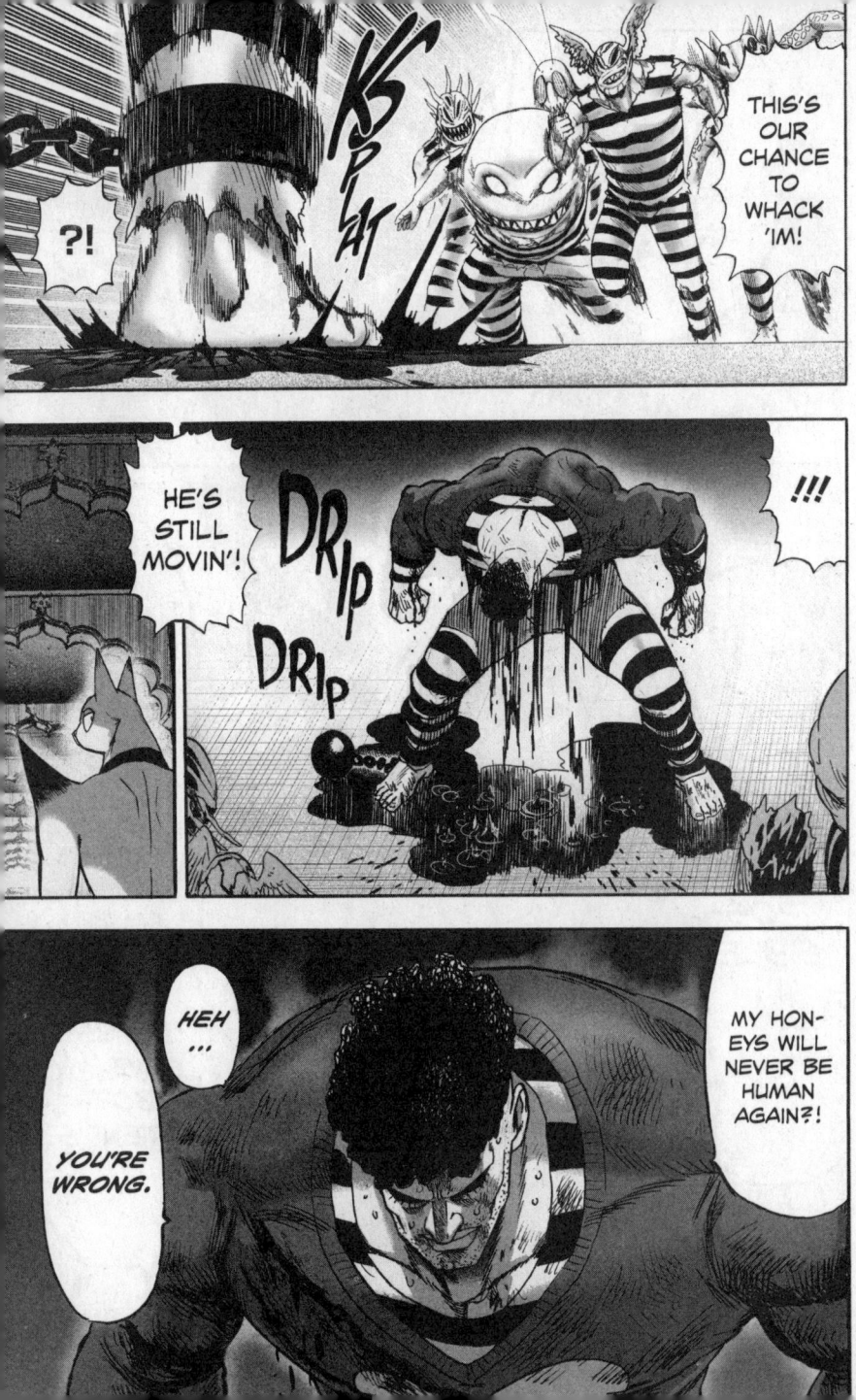
THIS'S OUR CHANCE TO WHACK 'IM!
KSPLAT
?!
!!!
HE'S STILL MOVIN'!
DRIP
DRIP
MY HONEYS WILL NEVER BE HUMAN AGAIN?!
HEH ...
YOU'RE WRONG.

ALL THAT MATTERS IS THE HUMAN HEART!

I WILL NEVER GIVE UP!
I MUST SAVE MY BOY-FRIENDS!
FOR LOVE, NOTHING IS IM-POS-SIBLE !!!
DA
DUM

ENOUGH! WE'LL NEVER CONVINCE HIM!
WE'RE NOT YOUR BOY-FRIENDS!
THAT SOUNDS ADMIRABLE, BUT HE'S TOTALLY CLUELESS!
KILL 'IM!
KILL 'IM!
IF HE WON'T FIGHT BACK, THAT'S ALL THE BETTER!
DID THE DAMAGE BUILD UP IN HIM, TRIGGERING A DEFENSIVE RESPONSE...
WHAT HAP-PENED?
...AND RAPID PHYSICAL EVOLUTION?!
WHAT THE HECK ?!
HE FEELS DIF-FERENT NOW!
?!

RMBL
RMBL
RMBL
RMBL
!

HAVE I GROWN ANGEL WINGS?
FWUF
NO! IT'S JUST BODY HAIR!

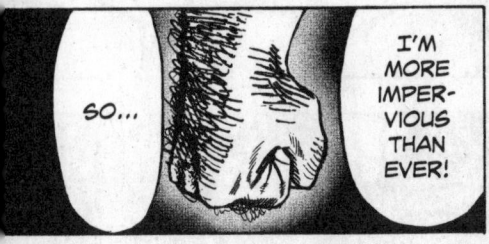
I'M MORE IMPERVIOUS THAN EVER!
SO...

I SHALL CALL IT...
...ANGEL ☆ BRISTLY ARMOR!

I'LL SAVE CUDDLING MY HONEYS UNTIL LATER...
...AND DEFEAT THAT CAT!!!

THIS FEELING OF REVUL-SION...
ULP!
...WHEN MY FORMER OWNER WOULD FORCE HER AFFECTION ON ME!
KISS
KISS
KISS
...JUST LIKE...
IT'S...
I'LL LEAVE HIM TO THE OTHER BIG SHOTS.
SWP
OH WELL.
AND THERE ARE CRACKS ALL OVER THIS PLACE!
I CAN FIT IN A SPACE ONLY THREE MILLI-METERS WIDE!
HOW DID HE FIT IN THERE ?!
?!

SEE YA!
SO I'LL GO KILL A DIFFERENT HERO.
WE'RE THE ONES ...
YO, PURI-PURI.
YOU WILL NOT ES-CAPE ME!
SMASH
GWUP
... WHO'RE GON-NA-
?!

ANGEL ☆ CRAWL!
I'LL SWIM THROUGH THE EARTH TO CHASE THAT CAT MONSTER!!!

SPROOOSH
THAT GUY'S MESSED UP.
...

I INSTINCTIVELY DETEST THAT GUY!
I CAN SENSE HIM APPROACHING!

SWIP

BASH
GEH!

SKROOOSH
MEOW?!

I LIVE A SELFISH EXISTENCE ...
...AND I ONLY FIGHT WHO I WANT.
SO GO FIGHT THOSE CONVICTS!
NO, I WILL FOLLOW YOU EVERY-WHERE!
SKROOSH
YOU SHAGGY BEAST!
SWIP
WHOA ...
YOU CAME BACK, MISTER NYAAN?
DIDJA SNUFF OUT PURI-PURI?
TMP
TMP

KRASHHH

OH NO !!!
I ACCIDEN-TALLY KILLED THEM!!!
MY BOY-FRIENDS! WAA-AAA-AAA-AAH!
BOO-HOO-OOO-OOO-OOO-OOO-OOO-OOO!

THANK YOU, MY HONEYS.
FWSH
FWSH
I ACCEPT MY NEW ABILITIES AS A GIFT FROM YOU.
URGH ...
YOUR SACRIFICE WILL NOT GO TO WASTE...
...SO WATCH OVER ME AS I FIGHT!

Venomous Lizard Sisters

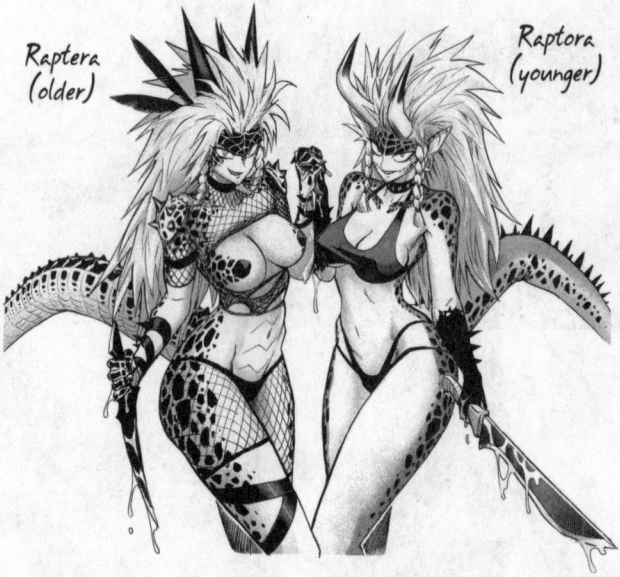

PUNCH 111: GLUTTONY

CHOMP CHOMP
LICK
CRUNCH
MUNCH MUNCH

...B-BUT...
CHOMP CHOMP
WE THOUGHT WE'D SUR-ROUND THIS HUNK OF MEAT AND MAKE A MEAL OF HIM...

GR
YIIIIKES!!!
AB

GULP GULP
...HE ATE EVERY-BODY!

H-HOW?! AREN'T YOU HUMAN?!
S-STOP! DON'T EAT ME!
WA-AA-AA-AA-AA-AA-AA-AH!

DMP
GW
GWP

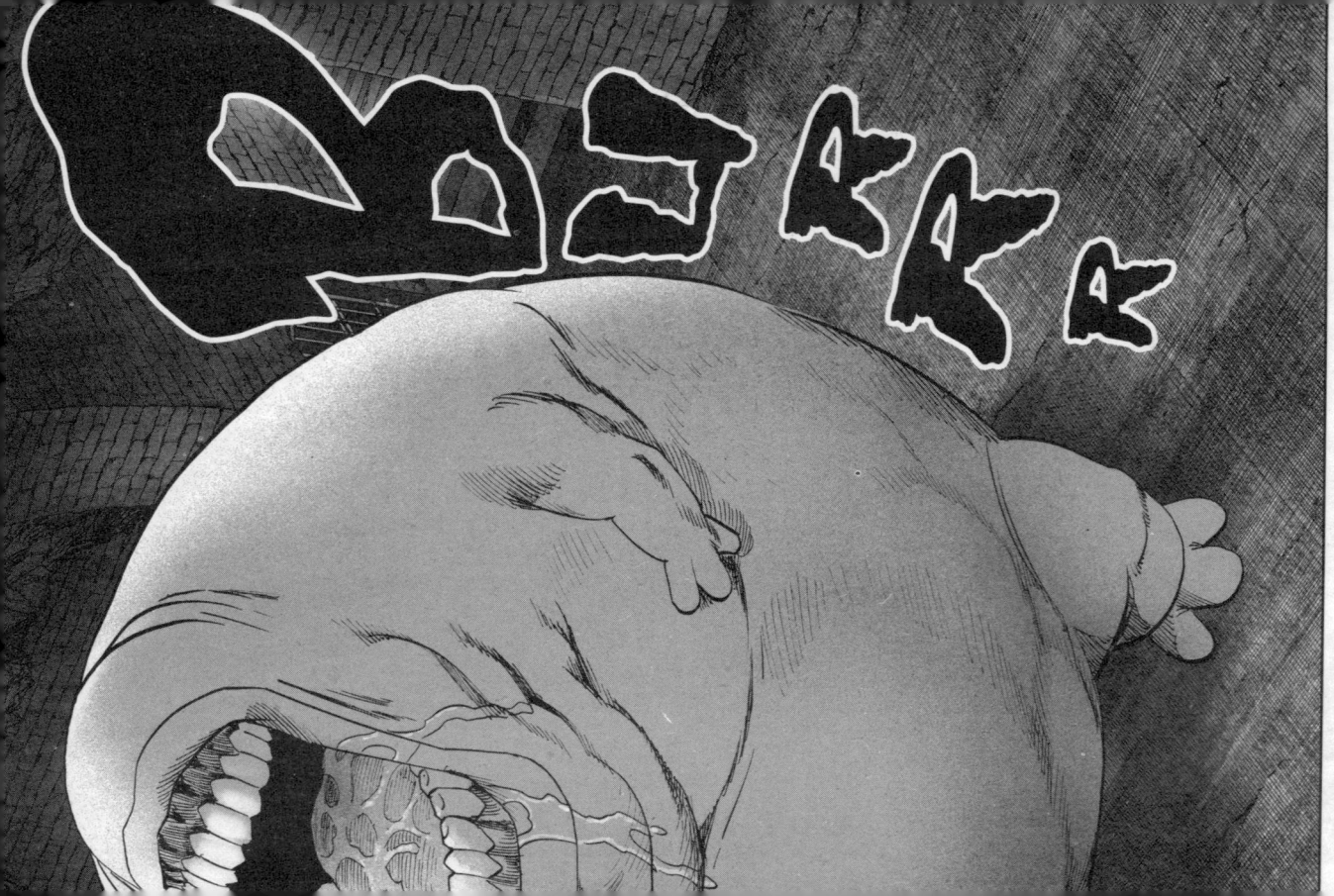
ごごごごご

Threat Level: Dragon

GUMS

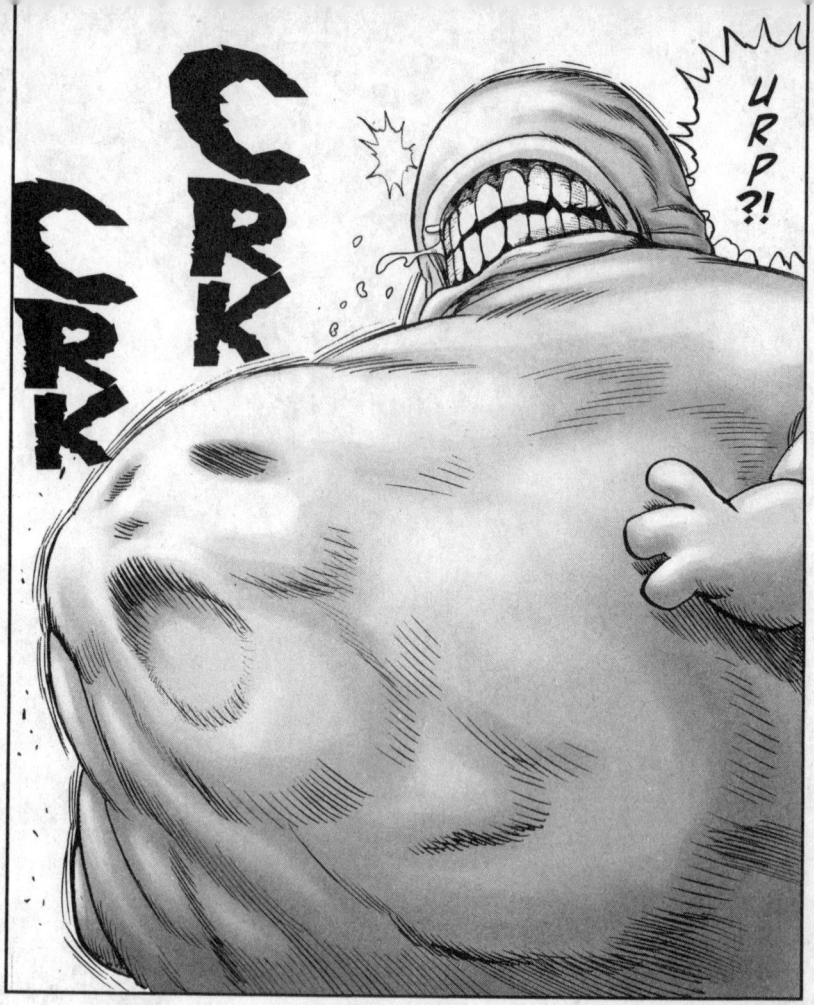
URP?!
CRK
CRK

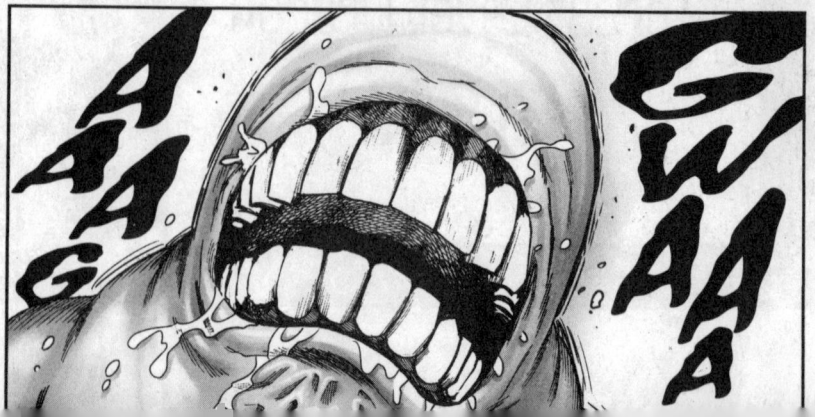
GWAAA
AAAG

BLOORRRCH
SPLUD
BLEE
EEAGH
WAP

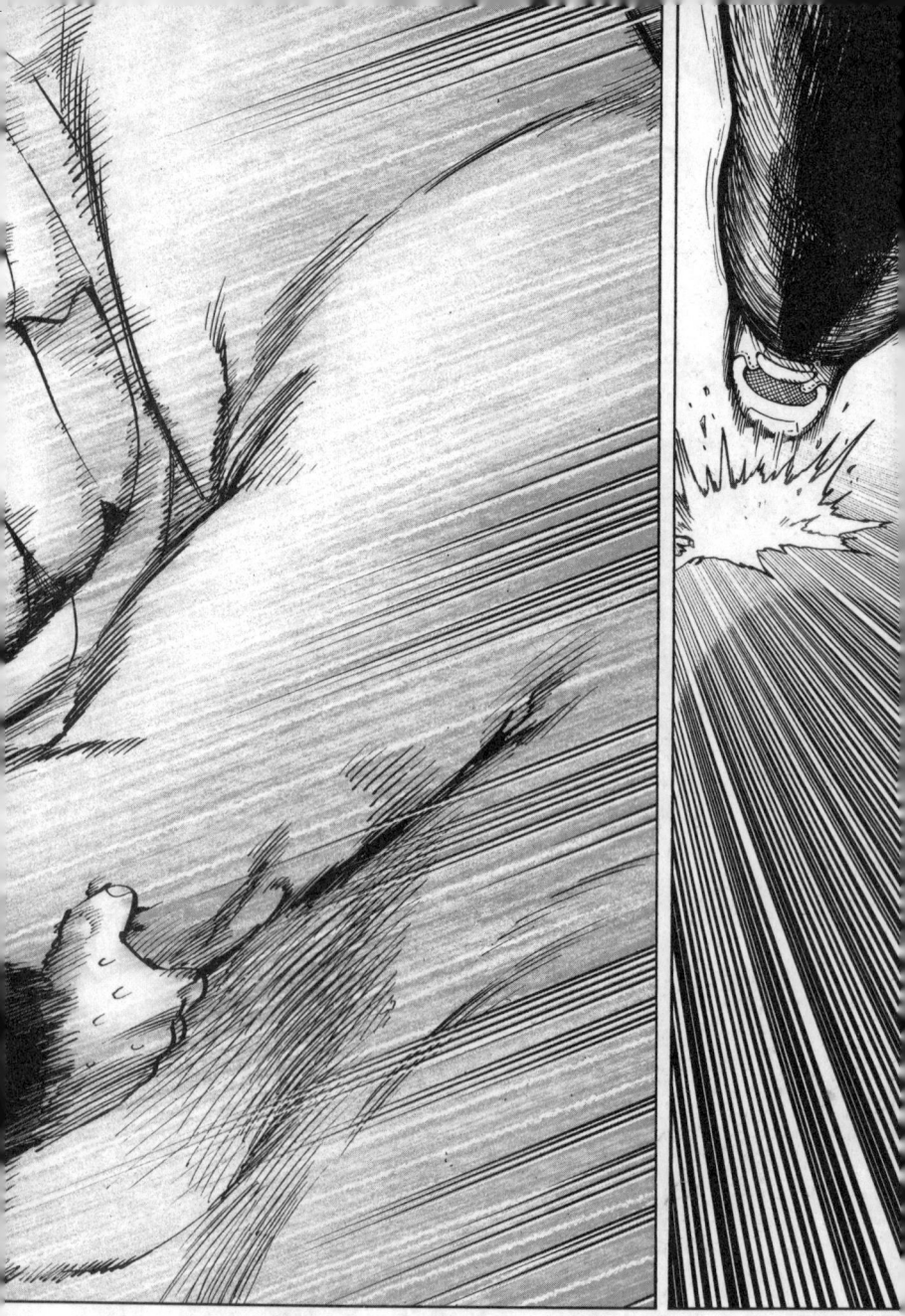

PUNCH 112:
SUPERALLOY BLACKLUSTER

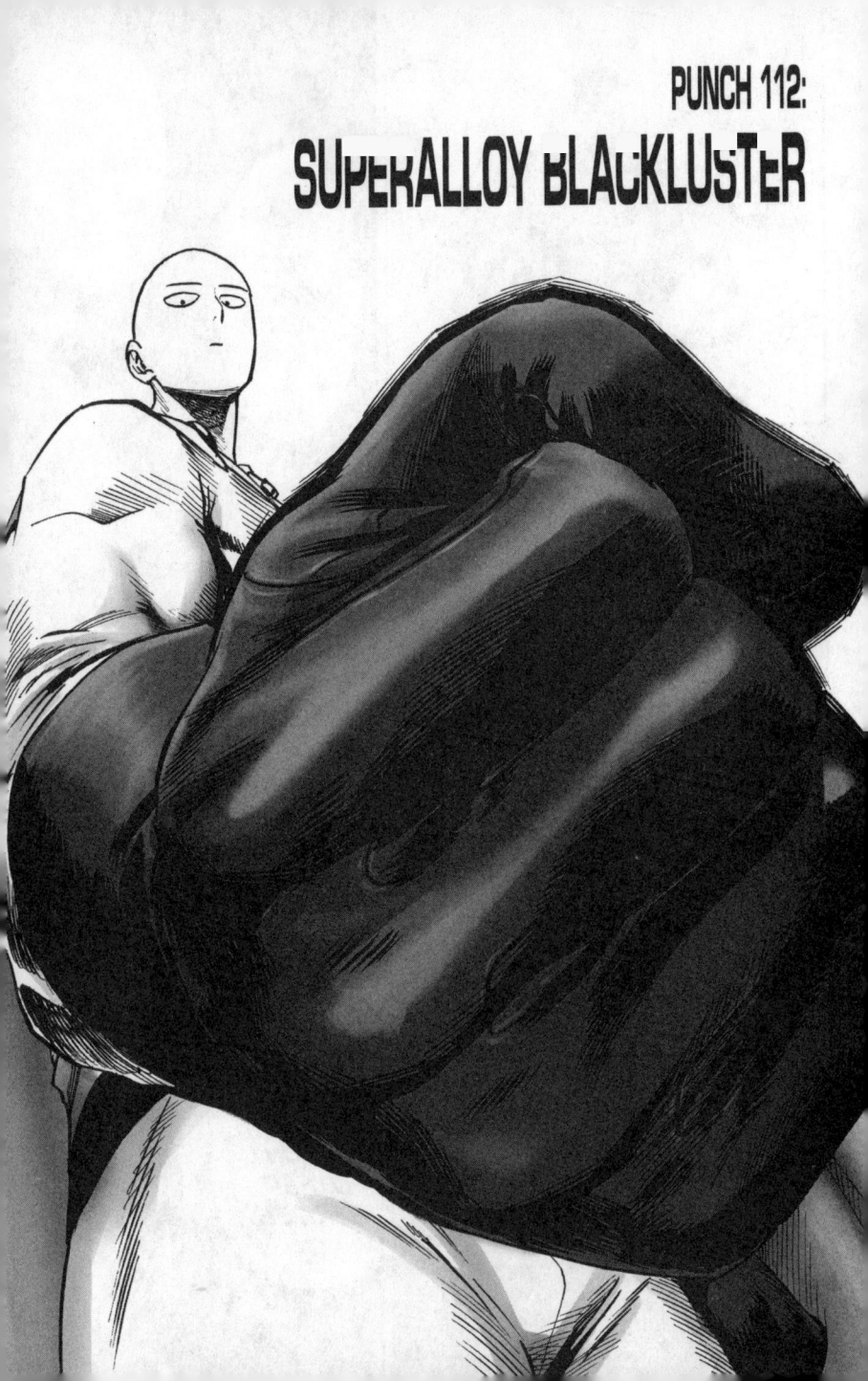

HEH...
THAT'S PRETTY DUMB.
CLOMP
...AND WISH HE HAD STUCK WITH ME!
HE'LL REGRET TAKING ON ANY HERO...
HMM...
THAT CAT SAID...
...IT WAS GOING TO HUNT OTHER HEROES.

SPZZAK
BWAM BWAM
THOOM
BWOOM

BROM
SKIDD
WHAM
BA BAM BAM
WHAT ARE YOU DOING?

WHY ARE YOU FREEZING UP?
HAVE YOU GIVEN UP?
SUPER-ALLOY BLACK-LUSTER ...
...WHY DON'T YOU FIGHT BACK?

...AN INDOMITABLE MANIFESTATION OF INSECT STRENGTH.
...YOU TOLD ME THAT YOU ARE...
INSECT GOD...
YOU'VE GOT THE POWER, SPEED AND FEROCIOUS STRENGTH OF AN INSECT GOD...
... BUT ...
IT WAS DISHEARTENING TO THINK A MONSTER HAD SURPASSED ME, SO I WANTED TO SEE WHAT YOU'VE GOT!
BUT THAT IS EXACTLY WHAT I HAVE STRIVEN TO BE!!!
YOU'RE A DISAPPOINTING INSECT MONSTER, BECAUSE YOU LACK THE BLACK LUSTER.
...YOU VASTLY FAIL TO MEET MY EXPECTATIONS.

YOU FOOL! DO NOT THINK THAT WAS A DISPLAY OF MY FULL-
I AM SORELY DISAP-POINTED!
JOLT
I'M WARNING YOU! THERE ARE THREE HEROES YOU MUST NEVER ANGER!
MY BODY IS NO MORE THAN EN-LARGED MUSCLE, BUT ITS PERFOR-MANCE OUT-CLASSES YOURS, INSECT GOD!

HER NAME IS TOR-NADO!
THEN THERE'S THE PSYCHIC CAPABLE OF UNTOLD SLAUGHTER!
TICK HER OFF, AND SHE'LL PULVERIZE YOU BEYOND RECOGNITION!
HIS NAME IS KING!
ONE IS THE STRONGEST CREATURE ON EARTH!
WHEN THE KING ENGINE RUMBLES, HE SENDS EVIL STRAIGHT TO HELL!
RMBL

FINALLY, THERE'S ME.
I'M SUPER-ALLOY BLACK-LUSTER, AND I SHINE WITH BLACK LIGHT!
WHEN I'M ANGRY, MY MUSCLES ACT ON THEIR OWN!
I SEE ...
WANT TO KNOW WHAT HAPPENS WHEN I'M ANGRY?

YOU HEROES HAVE FAILED TO DEFEAT THE HERO HUNTER, AND YET EVEN HIS FISTS WERE POWERLESS AGAINST ME.
CRRK
SNAP
POP
MY CARAPACE IS IMPENETRABLE ARMOR!
I EXIST ON A DIFFERENT PLANE THAN YOU MAMMALS BECAUSE MY INSECT MUSCLES INSTANTANEOUSLY IMPEL ME TO FULL POWER!
SNAP POP
KRAK

YOU MIGHT SAY MY WHOLE BODY IS A WEAPON!
I'M GONNA SHRED YOUR FAKE MUSCLES AND FEED 'EM TO THE BUGS!
THOSE ARE RECKLESS WORDS...

PI
I
IN
NNGGG
GRAWR!
I WILL BREAK YOU !!!!!

BADA
BABAM
BAM
BAM
BAM
BABAM
GRA-
AAR-
RRG-
GGH-
HH!

OP

PAW

BA
I TOLD YOU IT WAS RECK-LESS.
EVEN I DON'T KNOW HOW TO SCRATCH ME!
M
IF I DON'T FIGHT A BIG SHOT TOO, MY MUSCLES WILL LOSE THEIR MO-TIVATION.
HMM ...
TWITCH TWITCH
THAT SHAKING... IS SOME-ONE FIGHTING A TOP MON-STER?
BOOM
CRUMBL
CRUMBL
KATHO-OM
HM?

BONUS MANGA: SETTING AN EXAMPLE

Stop watching and help.
HOW COME YOU GRADE THE HEROES?
GULP
THIS GUY'S ANNOYING...
WELL, THAT'S HOW I FIGHT.
SO I HUNGER TO MAKE SURE YOU SATISFY MY STANDARDS.
LIKE I DO!
HEROES MUST PRESENT AN INSPIRING FIGURE.
I'M LIKE A TOP CHEF RATING RESTAURANTS.
A HUNGER YOU CAN'T CONTROL?
OH ...
HM ?
AWW, SHOW ME MY EVALUATION.
GIVE THAT BACK!
HEY, DON'T!
HWIP
WHATEVER.
AGH!

JOLT
THAT'S ODD.
SNATCH
BUT HE ALWAYS CRITICIZES MY SKILLS AND APPEARANCE.
BAN
Class S, R
Pig God
Abilities
Popularity
Personality
IT'S ALL ABOUT MY PERSONALITY.
GOT IT?! PART OF A HERO'S JOB IS SETTING A GOOD EXAMPLE!
I NEED TO, UM, ANALYZE EVERYONE TO IDENTIFY WHERE THEY NEED COACHING!
W-WELL, IT'S CRUCIAL ...
...TO RESEARCH WHO'S FIT TO BE A HERO.
SWEA SWEA
WHY'RE YOU SWEATING?
WHAT'S WITH THAT GUY?
HAHAHAHA
YOU PASS AGAIN, PIG GOD!
SEE YA!
FWOOSH
SO DON'T HESITATE TO FOLLOW MY LEAD!

!
SLURP
SLURP
FUMP
Backfat Ramen
0333XX1126
WEL-COME!
TAKE THE CHALLENGE!
Finish in 1 hr and it's FREE!
BELLY BUSTER
$5,000
SET AN EXAM-PLE, HUH?
Ugh... But I'm almost done!
...
PIG GOD!
BDUMP
HERE YA GO!
COMIN' UP!
BELLY BUSTER. TWENTY BOWLS, PLEASE.